Author:
David Stewart has written many non-fiction books for children. He lives in Brighton with his wife and son.

Artist:
David Antram was born in Brighton, England, in 1958. He studied at Eastbourne College of Art and then worked in advertising for fifteen years before becoming a full-time artist. He has illustrated many children's non-fiction books.

Series Creator:
David Salariya was born in Dundee, Scotland. He has illustrated a wide range of books and has created and designed many new series for publishers both in the UK and overseas. In 1989, he established The Salariya Book Company. He lives in Brighton with his wife, illustrator Shirley Willis, and their son Jonathan.

Editor: **Sophie Izod**

Consultant: **Stephen Johnson**
Director of Operations, Heritage Lottery Fund, and author of several books on Roman archaeology.

Published in Great Britain in 2006 by
Book House, an imprint of
The Salariya Book Company Ltd
25 Marlborough Place, Brighton BN1 1UB

ISBN 0-531-12423-1 (Lib. Bdg).
ISBN 0-531-12448-7 (Pbk).

Published in 2006 in the United States
by Franklin Watts
An imprint of Scholastic Library Publishing
90 Sherman Turnpike, Danbury, CT 06816

A CIP catalog record for this book is available from the Library of Congress.

Printed and bound in China.

You Wouldn't Want to Be a Roman Soldier!

At least we're seeing the world!

Barbarians You'd Rather Not Meet

Written by
David Stewart

Illustrated by
David Antram

Created and designed by
David Salariya

Franklin Watts®
A Division of Scholastic Inc.
NEW YORK • TORONTO • LONDON • AUCKLAND • SYDNEY
MEXICO CITY • NEW DELHI • HONG KONG
DANBURY, CONNECTICUT

Contents

Introduction

T:he year is A.D. 105 and the Roman Emperor Trajan is fighting against the barbarians on the Danube River in today's western Europe. You are Marius Gaius. At the age of 18, you joined the army to become a Roman soldier. The Roman army invades and conquers foreign lands to extend the frontiers of the empire. These lands are called provinces and all of them must send tributes and taxes to Rome. By the second century A.D. people living on the edge of the Arabian deserts, in north Africa, or in Britannia (Britain) can call themselves Roman citizens. As a Roman citizen who can speak Latin, you join the army as a legionary soldier. Joining the army will change your life forever and bring you hard work, danger, and excitement. Not everyone can join the army like you— slaves are not free to join. Soldier's pay varies from one unit to another. At the time of Emperor Hadrian (A.D. 117–138), legionary soldiers are paid about 300 silver denarii a year.

Map of the Roman Empire

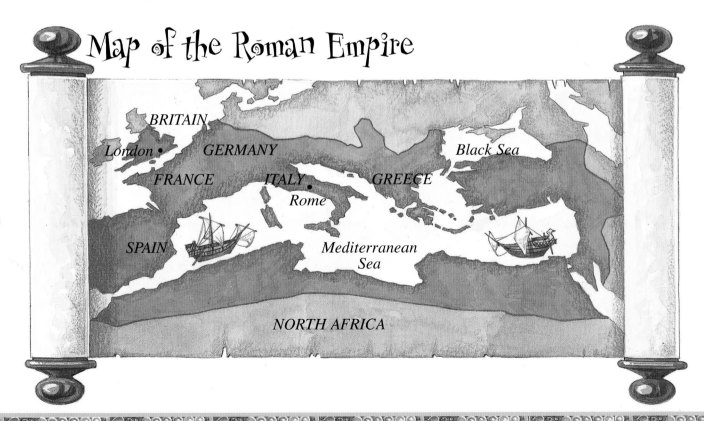

BRITAIN

London •

GERMANY

Black Sea

FRANCE

ITALY •

Rome •

GREECE

SPAIN

Mediterranean
Sea

NORTH AFRICA

Joining Up

A soldier's life is tough, so why would you want to enlist? You might die in battle or from diseases caught on campaign. Even when you are not fighting, you will spend long hours training or building roads and forts. Food is simple and discipline is harsh—so why become a soldier? One reason is that you will be paid fairly well and regularly. Soldiers also get a share of booty and a generous pension when they retire. There is a good chance of promotion, and it's a great way to escape a dull, routine life.

YOU CANNOT JOIN the army if you are a slave or if you are less than 5 1/2 feet tall. Sons of old soldiers are especially welcome. Once in the army, many men never see their homeland again.

As soon as I am tall enough, I am going to join the army!

You need to be 18 years old, too!

Swearing the Oath

THE MILITARY OATH. When you arrive at the recruitment camp you swear an oath that binds you to the army for 25 years, or until you die.

BUY YOUR UNIFORM. Equipment used by legionaries is mass produced in the eastern lands of the Roman Empire. The cost of your uniform, weapons, bedding, rations, a share in the tent, and the unit's burial fund will all be taken from your pay.

Legionary Infantry

Helmet

Armor made of metal strips

Supply kit

Sword

Leather stomach protector

Woolen tunic

Spear

Leather sandals

Handy Hint

You carry your own essential kit—a saw, a hook, a rope, a pick-axe, and much more. Make sure you pack carefully.

Cretan archer

Balearic slinger

Auxiliaries

AUXILIARY SOLDIERS were originally recruited from non-Roman tribes. Their name means "helpers," and they assist Roman legionary troops by providing extra manpower and specialized fighting techniques. They fight using armor and weapons from their native lands.

7

Training to Be a Legionary

A Roman legion is made up of...

8 men = 1 contubernium

10 contubernia = 1 century

2 centuries = 1 maniple

6 centuries = 1 cohort

T he Roman Imperial Army has about 150,000 soldiers, called legionaries, who join the army for life. They sign on for 25 years of service. Your army life begins with training in Rome. You are taught how to march and how to build a camp, and you must drill twice a day. Your main training is in the use of weapons and you are taught how to fight. You are in a group of eight men called a contubernium (a tent group). A century (80 men) is made up of ten such groups with a leader called a centurion.

Our word "military" comes from the Latin for soldier.

Road Building

ROMAN roads are built by ordinary soldiers. They form a vital network across the Roman Empire.

Horse riding!

Wrestling!

Swoooooosh!

Handy Hint
Remember your sword is still sharp along its edges. It's only the point that is covered!

LEGIONARIES are taught to ride, wrestle, and swim. Training battles are always dangerous and bloody. It's hard work but you survive . . . barely!

THE TRAINING GROUND. A post is set up for you to practice. You use real swords and spears, but the tips are covered.

Running!

We're supposed to be stabbing and thrusting at it!

He thinks he's chopping firewood!

10 cohorts = 1 legion (too many to fit on this page!)

Your First Battle

You and the other recruits are sent to the Danube—your first post abroad. Emperor Trajan has decided to enlarge the frontiers of the empire. The frontiers in this area have not changed since the time of the Emperor Augustus, 94 years ago, and Trajan thinks the time is right for another advance. He plans to declare war against the Dacians. This will act as a warning to those tribes outside the Roman Empire who think its lack of expansion is a sign of weakness. Drobeta is a wealthy Dacian city (in modern day Romania) on the Danube River. If captured it will provide the Imperial Treasury with a large profit.

War Machines:

Ballista

Much tougher than fighting with wooden posts!

Onager

ONAGER (left). Rocks are loaded into a sling fixed to a wooden arm. Twisting a rope will winch the arm back before being released and firing the rocks.

Handy Hint

Keep well clear when the onager is being fired — you could go with it!

BATTERING RAMS (left) knock holes in the enemy walls. Soldiers inside are well protected by the strongly made sides and roof.

Battering ram

Testudo (tortoise)

SOLDIERS (below) make a "tortoise" formation by overlapping their shields to form a strong defensive shell.

11

Return to Rome

You have survived your first real battle, and you are lucky to return from the Danube with Dacian prisoners and the treasures you captured. Every Roman loves a good show. One of the very best is when a triumphant army returns to Rome and puts on a triumph, or victory parade. The Roman emperor rides in a gilded chariot, and the procession winds through the streets and the Forum to the Capitol. This is where animals are sacrificed to the Roman gods Jupiter, Venus, Mars, and Victory. The chief prisoner (usually the enemy leader) may be executed.

Prisoners

PRISONERS (above) are sold in the slave market. Throughout the Roman empire there are millions of slaves who have no rights at all. Families are split up and sold separately. Strong, fit men are sold to be trained as gladiators (below).

Victory Parade:

THE STREETS OF ROME are packed with crowds. The senators lead the parade followed by row upon row of troops. Treasures captured in battle are carried shoulder high, and soldiers lead white oxen to be sacrificed at the Temple of Jupiter. The crowds cheer as enemy leaders are displayed in chains.

All at Sea

Time passes, but there is no rest for the soldiers. You have fought in many campaigns, and as an experienced soldier you are sent to Britannia (Britain). The Roman Empire has a new emperor now, Emperor Hadrian. It is Hadrian's policy not to expand the empire but to strengthen its existing frontiers. He wants his army to be highly efficient and is introducing reforms to make auxiliary troops serve far away from their country of origin.

Are we there yet?

The Imperial Navy

THE ROMAN NAVY plays its part in wars. Ships are used to carry men and horses to fight in distant lands. Julius Caesar had 600 special landing craft and 28 warships built to help with his invasion of Britannia in 54 B.C. But sea travel is difficult and has to be done during the summer.

Left, Right, Left, Right!

After a long sea journey you arrive in Britannia. You march north along roads built by other soldiers. Roads are built to suit the army, not the local people. They are usually as straight as possible, connecting important military centers. Soldiers march in strict order—cavalry at the front, then infantry, then the baggage train followed by the very best troops. It is necessary to make "marching camps," temporary overnight camps to rest in. Northern tribes have resisted the Roman invaders, and the previous legion that fought them has been wiped out. To stop the tribes attacking his troops and settlements, Hadrian has decided to build a long wall across the most easily defended part of Britannia.

We're on guard, so no tent for us tonight!

BASIC DIET is hard, dry bread with lard, washed down with vinegar or sour wine. When they're available you might also have lentils, beans, cabbage, mutton, lamb, beef, hare, goat, and deer. If you're lucky, you might even have some locally caught fish.

MARCHING makes the legionaries strong and fit. Distances of 20 miles must be covered at a quick pace in five hours. You would also carry 60 pounds of equipment.

SANDALS (right) have heavy studs on the soles to prevent the leather from wearing down quickly.

Handy Hint

Try to get a space in the middle of the tent. It's the warmest and driest position.

Tents are made of leather, with straw on the floor.

Hadrian's Wall

Once built, Hadrian's Wall is 73 miles long. It stretches from Bowness on the west coast of Britain to Wallsend in the east. The Wall is 15 feet high, 10 feet thick, and takes 6 years to complete! It is built by legionaries and marks the northern boundary of the vast Roman Empire. To the north of the Wall lies a deep defensive ditch designed to keep the unconquered tribesmen out, and to the south is a *vallum,* which is a large ditch flanked by huge mounds of earth. It is manned by 10,000 auxiliary soldiers from across the empire, and you're soon put to work building forts large enough to house men, horses, weapons, and supplies.

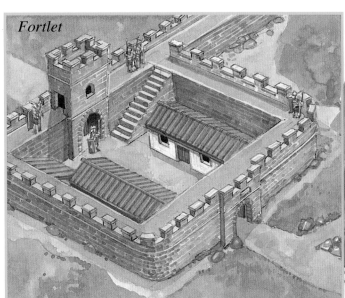

Fortlet

THERE ARE a total of 16 forts along the length of the Wall. Fortlets (above) are built every mile with signal towers every 580 yards between them.

EMPEROR HADRIAN ordered the building of the great wall after his visit to Britain in A.D. 122. The work began in the east.

Hadrian's Wall

Handy Hint

Ask a scribe to write home for underwear. Romans do not usually wear it, but a winter spent on the freezing wall soon changes old habits.

Brrrr

Life in the Fort

Luckily for you, once the Wall is complete you return to your well-appointed barracks in Chester, 100 miles to the south. Soldiers are not always fighting, so you have regular training sessions to keep fit. Life for legionaries and auxiliaries is much the same. Weapons need cleaning, animals need feeding, wood for fires needs cutting, and stoves need to be kept lit. The job of cleaning the latrines (bathrooms) is usually given as punishment, so try to avoid it!

Who's on latrine cleaning duties this week?

Keeping Clean:

ROMAN LATRINES (below). Seats are placed over a channel flushed with running water. Washable sponge sticks are used because there is no such thing as toilet paper yet!

BATH HOUSES. Bathing is an important part of Roman life all over the empire. Baths are a good place to meet friends, gossip, and relax.

Latrines

Baths

YOU SHARE two rooms in the fort barrack block with seven other men. One room is used for sleeping, and the other is for storing, cleaning, and repairing equipment. You all cook, eat, and relax there together.

Day-to-Day Life

Local people hated Hadrian's Wall and its forts when they were built. But they soon realized that there was money to be made from the newly arrived and relatively well-paid soldiers. Some local chiefs make an alliance with Rome to help fight their old tribal enemies. Villagers provide all kinds of services, from food and clothes to taverns to relax in. They also feel much safer being so close to such a large number of soldiers and are grateful that these troops—backed up by your legion's extra muscle when needed—can protect them from attack. No serving soldier in the Roman army is allowed to marry because of the long periods of time they must spend away from wives and children. However, many lonely soldiers choose local women as wives and rent houses outside the fort to live in and raise families. The army refuses to recognize these "unofficial" marriages until you complete your service, but everyone else does!

Getting Friendly:

A LOCAL GIRL catches your eye. After romancing her, the two of you fall head-over-heels in love.

NOT EVERYONE IS HAPPY for you, though. Your superiors disapprove and urge you to end the relationship.

MARRIED! Ignoring their advice, you wed the girl of your dreams. However, she will have to live outside the fort.

23

Battle the Barbarians!

A messenger arrives at your fortress. You and your fellow legionaries are needed to help defeat an attack by a large group of Brittones! It's a four-day march back to Hadrian's Wall, and you arrive to find a heated battle underway. In the front line, you hurl your spear at the enemy—a strong soldier can throw his spear over 80 feet —and then move in for hand-to-hand fighting using your sword. This is the most dangerous time for a Roman soldier, and many are injured. Before you know it, you too are wounded!

Who'd have thought it would end like this?

THE ROMANS and the Brittones both like collecting their enemies' heads as trophies.

Know Your Enemies:

Raaaargh!

Handy Hint

Avoid falling into enemy hands. Not all local ladies are kind and gentle.

THE TRIBES OF BRITTONES (Britons) make life on the frontier as difficult as possible for the Romans. They use ambushes and often attack in small groups before retreating so they don't get caught. Sometimes they even get inside a Roman fort and burn it down.

Illness and Injury

Each fort has a team of medical staff trained to provide emergency treatment and hospital care. Army doctors are highly respected and are assisted by dressers, who treat wounds during a battle and nurse the injured soldiers back to health. Common battle wounds include jagged sword cuts, broken bones, and dislocated joints. Doctors clean wounds and stitch them together. They also sometimes have to amputate damaged limbs. Salt, turpentine, and arsenic are used as antiseptics to keep wounds from becoming infected. You're in good hands because Roman army doctors can give you excellent medical care.

2

3

SPEAR POINTS and arrowheads (below) sunk deep into the flesh are difficult to remove and treat.

DRESSERS give first aid on the battlefield.

WELL-PLANNED HOSPITALS are an essential part of every fort (right). As well as having operating tables and beds for soldiers to recover on, they also prepare all the medicines and bandages here.

Medical Instruments

1. Spatula (knife for spreading ointment)
2. Tweezers
3. Probe used for shallow wounds
4. Hook
5. Knife used for surgery
6. Forceps

Handy Hint

Drink alcohol as a way to numb pain during surgery. Be careful though—alcohol thins your blood so you will bleed more.

GRIMACE AND BEAR IT. Bite down on a piece of wood as the doctor operates to stitch and clean the wound. It's agony, but there is no anesthetic to numb the pain.

LUCKILY YOU make a full recovery, and your wife and son welcome you home. Any soldiers too weak to fight are retired.

Promotion, Retirement, Death

After a full recovery you return to army life, and soon your mind turns to promotion. As you come from an ordinary Roman family, you must work hard to prove you have what it takes to become a legionary centurion—one of the most important ranks in the army. This means showing skill and courage in battle as well as leadership. You'll never achieve the highest rank in the army, though —that belongs to the emperor!

AS WELL AS FIGHTING, centurions have daily meetings to report any problems and are responsible for ordering fresh supplies.

PASSWORDS. Roman forts were targets for enemy spies. To stop them from infiltrating the fort, change the *tessera*, or password, daily (below).

Two Ways to Become a Centurion

THE EASY WAY. Be born into a wealthy family.

THE HARD WAY. Start at the bottom and work your way up.

AVCRIB

*Signifier
(standard bearer)*

*Legatus
(commander
of a legion)*

Tribune (staff officer)

Handy Hint

It's been so long since you left home that there's no point in returning—nobody would remember you!

Rank and File:

ON YOUR journey up the career ladder you have been both a tribune and a standard bearer, but sadly you never made legatus. If you had, you could have been made governor of a Roman province when you retired.

REMEMBERED. When you die, your proud son erects a tombstone in your honor.

What Can You Look Forward To?

SHARE A DRINK and swap stories with other retired soldiers and friends.

GIFT OF LAND. After 25 years of service and numerous scars, you retire honorably. The army gives you some land on which you can build a home and start a farm. But farming is hard work—there's no time to relax for you!

Glossary

Alliance An agreement to cooperate between two or more groups of people.

Amputate To cut off a limb when it is badly damaged.

Anesthetic A substance that reduces the feeling of severe pain.

Antiseptic Something that reduces the likelihood of infection by killing germs.

Arsenic A very poisonous substance used by Romans to treat infections. It is very dangerous.

Auxiliary Soldiers recruited from local areas either inside or outside the Roman Empire.

Ballista A large catapult used to hurl objects such as spears or rocks at enemies.

Barbarian The name given to another nation or civilization the Romans considered more primitive.

Booty Treasure captured from an enemy during war.

Britannia The Roman name for Britain.

Brittones The Roman name for the tribes in the area of Hadrian's Wall.

Century A unit of 80 men in the Roman army.

Dacians People from what is now Romania.

Danube A river that flows through a number of countries in Europe. It was one of the frontiers of the Roman Empire.

Denarii Roman units of currency.

Forum An important meeting place in ancient Rome.

Laurel A bush whose leaves were used to make wreaths worn on the head to celebrate a victory. Only important Romans could wear them.

Legatus The commander of a legion; a highly skilled and experienced officer.

Legionary A soldier in an army unit of about 4,800 soldiers.

Onager A device like a catapult that fired rocks at enemies.

Scribe Someone paid by the soldiers to write letters home. Many Roman soldiers could not read or write.

Tessera A Latin word meaning "password."

Triumph The name of the victory procession through Rome after an important battle had been won.

Turpentine A liquid made from the resin of trees that was used to treat infections. It is very dangerous and is not used as medicine today.

Index